D1558709

THIMBLE
AMERICANA

❦

And Contemporary Collectibles

Myrtle Lundquist

On the Cover (Top Left): "Christmas Remembered."
Washington at Prayer, Valley Forge. (Top Right): Liberty
Bell inscribed "PROCLAIM LIBERTY IN THE LAND TO
THE INHABITANTS BY ORDER OF THE ASSEMBLY OF
PENNSY. IN PHIL'A. 1752." (Lower Left): "The Signing of
the Declaration of Independence by Delegates of the Thirteen
United States of America, July 4, 1776." From the painting
by John Trumbull. (Center): the Statue of Liberty presented
by the people of France in 1876. The border depicts the sky-
line of New York. (Right): Pilgrims at Plymouth Colony,
1621, celebrating the first Thanksgiving.

Copyright©1981
Myrtle Lundquist

Library of Congress
Catalog Number 80-50109

ISBN 0-87069-326-3

Published by

Wallace-Homestead Book Company
1912 Grand Avenue
Des Moines, Iowa 50309

Contents

Acknowledgments

The assistance of the following and all who contributed thimble expertise is gratefully acknowledged:

Mrs. Elizabeth Barker

Mrs. Roz Belford

Mrs. William Blackburn

Mrs. Martin Bloomquist

Mrs. Natalie Borg

Mrs. Leona Coad

Mrs. Josephine Collins

Mrs. Ray Conn

Mrs. Grace Cottrell

Mrs. Lorraine M. Crosby

Mrs. Teresa Cullen

Mrs. Dreme Davis

Mrs. Betty Dierdorf

Mrs. Cecile Dreesmann

Mrs. Evelyn Eubanks

Mrs. George Fisher

Mrs. Wilson Forker

Mrs. Ruby Gallacher

Mrs. Lahoma Goldsmith

Mrs. Pearl Hazen

Mrs. Yvonne Hecht

Mrs. William Hunt

Mrs. Leasa Jennish

Mrs. Dorothy Mager

Mr. Milton Mager

Mrs. Sandy McFadyen

Mrs. Betty Michaels

Mrs. Paula Moore

Mrs. Shirley Newton

Mrs. M. Adelle Puetz

Mrs. John Rich

Mrs. Edgar Sampson

Mrs. Nina Tillman Vaughn

Mrs. Vi Waite

Mrs. William B. Weiss

Mrs. Fred N. Whiting

Mrs. Lina Mae Whiting

Ms. Carol Winandy

Mrs. Charles Zabriskie

T. J. Cullen, Jeweller
The Franklin Mint
Collector Circle

List of Illustrations

Introduction

"Greatness is measured by the high uses
to which we devote humble things."
(Author unknown. From old prayer book)

This book is dedicated to collectors of thimbles with acknowledgment to those who have contributed to data thus far acquired.

Thimbles are a newly-tapped source of complex data pertaining to many fields. A sampling of classifications delineates various avenues of research. Hundreds of thimbles are photographed for reference.

History, cultures, art, and metalsmithing are some of the disciplines a collector may trace through the study of thimbles.

From early times, everywhere a form of thimble took part in family lifestyles and improvement of a social structure.

Thimbles have not varied in shape a great deal over the centuries. The purpose, to cap and protect a finger, remains the same.

Thimble collectors may trace cultures through the study of metals, design, geographical origin, and craftsmanship.

It is the purpose of this book to share some of the data suggested by thimble collectors who add much to the Americana of local history.

Besides considering tangible data, it is the purpose also to inspire reflection on the courage and character of those who used thimbles in former times.

To improve the quality of life is the inherent purpose for use of thimbles. Those who study them are enriched.

Part One

Thimble Americana

Sewing is motivated by the desire
to enhance the quality of life.
This is the universal urge that
the use of thimbles implies.

Collecting Thimbles

Thimble collecting is for everyone, men and women, young and old.

By definition a thimble is a small, cap-like sewing tool used to protect the finger and facilitate sewing.

Thimbles have not varied a great deal over the centuries. The basic shape does not change. Collectors who become fascinated by thimbles soon discover that cultures may be traced through wide areas of study. This is the inspiration for research.

There is hardly a medium imaginable from which a thimble has not been made. The diversified materials present a challenge to most collectors.

Artistry, craftsmanship, design, media, color, and maker are a few characteristics through which a collector may identify thimbles.

The Intangible Appeal

Anyone who knows what a thimble is and its use, revives personal associations. This is the intangible appeal of thimbles which fascinates collectors. This is the emotion aroused by considerations of past generations.

One thimble with some personal attachment may be the item that leads to collection of hundreds of thimbles and a lifetime interest in bridging the past with what is to come. This piece may have belonged to a grandmother or mother or other beloved person. A chain of family events evokes personal pride in the memory of successes and progress. There is something special about an heirloom thimble. To trace the beginning of a collection is often as absorbing as the items involved.

Collectors who accumulate large quantities of thimbles classify groups for comparison or convenience, starting with representative examples.

Old thimbles contribute data pertaining to many fields. The study of one old thimble may pursue metals, identification of marks, periods of style, industrial uses and policies, craftsmanship and artistry. There seems to be no limit to avenues of research revealing the imaginative progression of thimbles.

For the history enthusiast, thimble Americana is part of a search that may long continue. History is always in the making and thimbles afford pursuits through a wide variety of skills and craftsmanship.

Special Interest Categories

Advanced collectors frequently focus on a category of some special interest. This preference might include

Animals	Inscriptions
Borders	Locations
Brass	Names
Commemorative	Patents
Dates	Patriotic
Design	Porcelains
Enamels	Religious
Flowers	Scenic
Foreign	Scrimshaw
Gold	Souvenir
Historical	Sterling

Arrangement, display, and research are left to the innovative collector.

The Texture of History

History as a special category sends collectors searching in depth, far and wide. Location, economy of the times, and social patterns must be considered in identifying an item. There is something exhilarating about examining a thimble that existed through times past. Americana is well represented in most thimble collections.

Some thimbles in collections today were handy when there was a McGuffey Reader on a table and perhaps a Currier and Ives print on the wall. Meeting houses and quilting bees were social centers. Early communication was by wagon train, water routes, and the Pony Express. Children learned the alphabet and proverbs stitching samplers.

Peddlers

In the eighteenth and nineteenth centuries, along the frontier, itinerant peddlers sold notions and fabrics from one-horse wagons with built-in shelves.

Covered Wagons

Covered Conestoga wagons carried thimbles for domestic use across the plains. Some were keepsakes with reminiscent inscriptions: "Remember Me," "Forget-Me-Not."

Home Magazines

Home magazines contained patterns for the latest fashions in clothing and needlework. Women created beautiful handwork. Their menfolk built furniture.

Revolutionary War

The West Point Museum at the United States Military Academy, West Point, New York, retains in the Revolutionary War display a few small fragments of thimbles excavated near the major encampments and fortifications of West Point.

Paul Revere

A gold thimble now in the Boston Museum of Fine Arts, Boston, Massachusetts, was made about 1805 by Paul Revere for his daughter, Marie Revere Balestier.

It is probable that all early American silversmiths produced custommade thimbles. Some who are known to have made and advertised thimbles were: Benjamin Halsted, Charles Shipman, Ketcham and McDougall of New York; James Peters of Philadelphia; George, David and Nathan Platt, and Ezra Prime of Huntington, L.I.

Simons Bros.

Simons Bros. of Philadelphia were in the thimblemaking business in the 1830s and are still making thimbles today.

Brigham Young, 1801 – 1877

A thimble used by Brigham Young to mend his tent during the westward travel of Mormons is preserved at Temple Square Museum, Salt Lake City, Utah.

Andersonville, Georgia, 1863

In the scrimshaw category, there is one thimble carved "Andersonville 1863" which might send a collector to study a prison and thousands of prisoners of the Civil War. Old records might reveal whether "M.D.W." survived.

Atlantic Cable, 1866

A thimble now in the Science Museum, London, was used as a small battery to send the first signals across the Atlantic Ocean by cable.

The Golden Spike, 1869

The Golden Spike was driven at Promontory Point, in northern Utah, May 10, 1869, to commemorate the joining of the Central Pacific and Union Pacific railroads at that spot. The St. Louis Fair souvenir thimble depicts the iron horse and is sometimes called "The Golden Spike."

World Columbian Exposition, Chicago, 1893

The 1893 World's Fair brought visitors from around the world to view industrial exhibits. Two thimbles by Simon Bros. commemorate the Fair.

Campaign Thimbles

Since the 1920s, presidential campaign thimbles have been issued as follows:

Coolidge-Dawes	Carter
Hoover-Curtis	Nixon
Hoover	Vote Straight Republican Ticket
LaFollett-Wheeler	McGovern-Shriver
Roosevelt-Garner	Willkie

Golden Spike Thimble

At right is a photograph of the official thimble issued in 1904 as a souvenir of the St. Louis World's Fair, sometimes called the Louisiana Purchase Exposition, celebrating the 100th anniversary of the purchase of the northern part of Louisiana by the United States from France. Forty-two states and fifty nations participated.

Depicted on the border are figures familiar during the opening of the west. Included are buffalo, men and horses, a covered wagon, a canoe representing water transportation and portages, and the steam iron horse.

This thimble has been called "The Golden Spike" as the drawing could indicate the completion and meeting of the Central Pacific and Union Pacific railroads. May 10, 1869, a golden spike was driven at Promontory Point in northern Utah to commemorate the occasion.

Part Two

Classifications

"It is perhaps a more fortunate
destiny to have a taste for collecting
shells than to be born a millionaire."
Robert Louis Stevenson

There are no identical thimble collections. All contain some items found in other groups and each contains thimbles of exclusive design or heritage.

A collection in a way embodies the taste, philosophy, and character of the collector.

There is no class distinction among thimbles. A heavy old brass inscribed "Remember Me" might have belonged to a dear relative. A platinum thimble set with rubies represents another set of values. Both are distinctive.

Between these poles are many gradations of classification.

Categories

Animals	Iron
Borders	Ivory
Campaign	Jeweled
Children's	Leather
Cupids	Mother of Pearl
Commemoratives	Names
Dates	Panels
Dorcas	Panoramic
Enamel	Patents
Floral	Patriotic
Foreign	Religious
Fruit	Scenic
Geographical	Scrimshaw
Geometric	Silk (Korean)
Historical	Simons
Holidays	Souvenir
Indentations	States (50)
Indian	Sterling
Initials	Stone Tops
Inscriptions	Wood

12

Animals
Pets appeared on some early thimbles, notably Gabler Brothers designs.

Borders
Borders afford space for decoration, including settings, enamel, and engraving. Popular patterns included beading, bright-cut, chasing, cut-card work, egg and dart, embossing, feather edge, fluting, gadroon, lattice, lozenge, lotus leaf, medallion, pierced work, repoussé, ribbon cut, rolled rim, scallops, scroll, strapwork, swag (drapery or festoons) of flowers.

Commemoratives
Commemoratives are a type of souvenir which record a date or special event. (Many examples were issued for the bicentennial celebration of 1976.)
World Columbian Exposition 1492 – 1892, Chicago.
Philadelphia Sesquicentennial 1776 – 1926.
Golden Gate International Exposition, 1939, San Francisco. Shows Bay
    Area and Golden Gate Bridge.
Liberty Bell on enamel. 1976. (Bicentennial)
Signing of the Declaration of Independence, 1776 – 1976 (Bicentennial).
    Embossed collected delegates signing the historic document.

Dorcas Thimbles
Dorcas thimbles, made by Charles Horner, patented in 1884, contain a layer of steel sandwiched between the inner silver lining and the outer silver covering. Early Dorcas thimbles bear no identifying mark but will respond to a magnet.

Indentations
Indentations may be hand-pounced or machine turned. These are easily distinguished by the regularity of knurled patterns or irregularity of hand-pitted rows. Patterns may be

round	square
hexagonal	diamond
teardrop	floral
and combinations.	

Panels
In the late 1800s, panels were a popular style. Thimbles with a variety of panels were made by many silversmiths. The number of panels, placing of design on each, or on every other panel, or between panels, identify a wide variety of thimbles of the period.

Religious
Many modern thimbles with a religious theme are handpainted. Churches and shrines are attractive motifs.

Scenic

Early thimbles made along the Atlantic seaboard depicted the sea and lighthouses. Silversmiths farther west engraved farm scenes. Villages, houses, bridges, boats, water, mountains, and churches decorated many thimbles. Some scenes or buildings may be identified.

Silk

Korean thimbles shaped like a small tea cozy were made of silk and other fabrics.

Porcelain

In the 1700s, exquisite porcelain thimbles were made by the Meissen studios in Germany. Miniature paintings on thimbles of the period record common scenes of the times.

Modern colorful thimbles are produced by renowned porcelain houses.

England	Ashleydale
	Caverswall
	Coalport
	Hammersley
	Royal Adderley
	Royal Crown Derby
	Royal Worcester
	Spode
	Wedgwood
France	Haviland
	Limoges
Germany	Bareuther
	Dresden
Hungary	Herend
	Hollohaza
Norway	Porsgrund
Denmark	Royal Copenhagen

Patents

Design patents are issued for drawings of artistic or souvenir type thimbles.

Regular or "Letters" patents for thimbles are granted to protect inventors of innovations. Among these are threaders, cutters, pushers, magnets, and a variety of attachments.

Scrimshaw

Scrimshaw is the folk art form of whalemen of the eighteenth and nineteenth centuries. Sailors who carved whalebone were called scrimshanders.

Since whales are now a protected species, elephant ivory and bone are modern substitutes.

Carving on whalebone during three and four year whaling voyages has come to be known as scrimshaw.

For their own use, whalers made whalebone tools such as awls, lures, and other articles to substitute for wood or metal.

Designs, pictures, and sentiments were carved on gifts for the home folks, wives, or sweethearts. Workboxes, bodkins, needlecases, seam rollers, and thimbles for the ladies have survived.

John Fitzgerald Kennedy was a collector of scrimshaw. He had been a naval hero and interested always in history. The pieces in his collection are large whale teeth decorated with historical figures.

During the Civil War, thousands of Union soldiers were imprisoned at Andersonville Prison in Georgia, now a national historic site. A thimble carved there by "MWM" marked "Andersonville 1863" is shown in the photographed scrimshaw category.

(The photograph of scrimshaw thimbles is used through the courtesy of Mrs. Paula Moore.)

Souvenir

Souvenir thimbles depict a place of interest without reference to a particular occasion.

"Brooklyn Bridge" (Patented 1881)

"Florida" (Patented 1881)

"Mount Vernon" with George Washington's plantation

"New York Subway" with tunnel and train

"Portland Oregon 1927"

"Salem – 1692" Issued for 200th anniversary in 1892. Known as the Salem Witch thimble, with witch, cat, new moon on band.

"St. Augustine Florida" (Patented 1881). Coat of arms. "Settled in 1565."

"St. Augustine" (Unmarked). Alligator, City Gate.

"Washington D.C." (Simons). White House and Capitol in ovals, separated by Washington monument. (Patented 1893.)

Advertisements

Plastic, aluminum, brass, and other thimbles with advertising may well become collectors' items of the future and sources of data.

A thimble depicting a dinosaur was issued by Sinclair Oil Company, no longer in business under that name.

Color Section

Representative categories illustrated in photographs that follow were assembled from private collections or furnished through the courtesy of Collector Circle and The Franklin Mint.

Americana

Top row: (1) George Washington at prayer. (2) Pilgrims' Thanksgiving. (3) Signing of the Declaration of Independence. (4) Liberty Bell. (5) Statue of Liberty.

Second row: (1) Betsy Ross. (2) Mount Vernon. (3) Flag. (4) Buildings of Washington, D.C. (5) Spirit of '76.

Third row: (1) San Francisco Exposition, 1939. (2) St. Louis Fair, 1904. Sometimes called The Golden Spike. (3) Space Needle, Seattle Fair, 1962. (4) Sesqui-Centennial, Philadelphia, 1776-1926. (5) Molly Pitcher. Battle of Monmouth.

Fourth row: (1) Thomas Jefferson. (2) Paul Revere. (3) Bi-Centennial, 1776-1976. (4) Independence Hall. (5) George Washington.

Fifth row: Campaign thimbles: (1) Coolidge-Dawes. (2) Hoover-Curtis. (3) Hoover. (4) La Follette-Wheeler. (5) Roosevelt-Garner.

Sixth row: Campaign thimbles: (1) Carter. (2) Nixon. (3) Vote Straight Republican Ticket. (4) McGovern-Shriver. (5) Willkie.

Scrimshaw

The use of this photograph and data from the collection of Paula Moore is gratefully acknowledged.

During the nineteenth century, hundreds of whaling vessels carried whalemen on three-to-five year voyages hunting whales. Monotony motivated scrimshandering, the carving of whalebone. Gifts for wives or sweethearts were decorated with hearts, sentiments, and drawings.

Prisoners of war, some of whom may have been sailors, passed time by carving names, dates, and sentiments on small objects of bone.

In 1863, thousands of Civil War prisoners were held at Andersonville, Georgia. A thimble carved there records some of that history. (Row 9, #3.)

Top row: (1) Whalebone thimble decorated with whale. (2) Whale ivory thimble with whale rising out of ocean. (3) Whale ivory with whale carved in relief.

Second row: (1) Front side of ivory thimble shows lighthouse; reverse side shows tail of great whale disappearing in the sea. (2) Whaling vessel decorates front of thimble; whale breaking water on reverse. (3) Whale ivory thimble decorated with ship's anchor.

Third row: (1) Whale ivory with eagle holding banner which reads "E. Pluribus Unum." (2) Ivory thimble dated 1876 is inscribed "Lila" on reverse. (3) Ivory thimble inscribed "Unum E. Pluribus."

Fourth row: (1) Two hearts pierced by a single arrow, "May – Ted." (2) Hearts formed by needle indentations on a bone thimble. (3) More hearts on an ivory thimble.

Fifth row: (1) Made of ivory for the recipient, "Enid Nye." (2) Large ivory thimble with large hearts. (3) Whalebone heart inscribed "I Love You"; a bouquet of posies on reverse side.

Sixth row: (1) Flower-wreathed heart for "Mother" on whalebone.)2) Large thimble of whalebone made for "Mother." (3) Memories of a far-away home inspire picture on one side of bone thimble; "Home Sweet Home" is inscribed on reverse.

Seventh row: (1) Three hearts strung on elongated arrow to "Susan From Papa, 1871." (2) "I Love You Bess" signed "Tim" on bone thimble. (3) Deeply carved ivory thimble made especially for "Millie."

Eighth row: (1) Heavily incised ivory thimble. (2) Thimble decorated with heart, club, diamond, and spade. (3) Ivory thimble with tropical isle scene on one side, whaling vessel on reverse.

Ninth row: (1) Rare shape bone thimble. (2) Unusual rectangular shape ivory thimble for "Susan." (3) Most unusual bone thimble of collection, made in Andersonville Prison by captured whaler "M.D.W.," dated 1863.

Commemoratives

Commemorative thimbles are souvenirs which record a date or special event.

Top row: (1) Constitution Hall. (2) Golden Gate International Exposition, San Francisco. (3) Coronation Commemoration Victoria, 1837 – 1897. (4) World's Columbian Exposition, 1492 – 1892, Chicago. (5) World's Columbian Exposition, 1492 – 1892.

Second row: (1) Bicentennial 1776 – 1976 on shield. (2) Castle scene, enamel. (3) Queen Elizabeth Silver Jubilee, 1952 – 1977. (4) Ricordo D'oropa. (5) Bicentennial 1976, Liberty Bell on enamel.

Third row: (1) Brooklyn Bridge. (2) Mines Metallurgy Building, Jamestown Exposition, 1607 – 1907. (3) 400th Anniversary, Discovery of America, 1492 – 1892. (4) Westminster Abbey. (5) Sesqui-Centennial, Philadelphia, 1776 – 1926.

Fourth row: (1) Liberty Bell, by Simons. (2) Liberty Bell, gold, by Simons. (3) Liberty Bell on shield. (4) Old Liberty Bell. (5) Liberty Bell charm.

Souvenir

Souvenir thimbles are mementoes of places of interest.

Top row: (1) Castle. Unmarked. Dated September 20, 1881. (2) St. Augustine, Fla. (3) Valley Forge, Pa. (4) Gettysburg, Pa. (5) Mount Vernon.

Second row: (1) Basilica De Fatima, Portugal. (2) Souvenir. (3) Heidelberg, Germany. (4) Bermuda. (5) Vineyard Haven.

Third row: (1) Ohio. (2) New Zealand. (3) Schmuckmuseum, Pforzheim, Germany, 1978. (4) Suva Fiji. (5) Madrid.

Fourth row: (1) Buckingham Palace. (2) Houses of Parliament. (3) Edinburgh Castle. (4) Worcester Cathedral. (5) London.

Scenes

Early scenic thimbles made along the Atlantic coast pictured the sea and lighthouses. Silversmiths farther west engraved village or farm scenes.

Top row: (1) Row houses. (2) Houses and churches. (3) Houses and trees. (4) Sailboat, lighthouse. (5) Houses, silo. (6) Cathedral towers.

Second row: (1) Village scene. (2) Repousse scene. Patented. (3) Mountain, cabin, trees. (4) House. No rim. (5) Castle. (6) Island and house.

Third row: (1) Houses, lighthouse. (2) Simons. Flowers, house. (3) (Gold) Simons. Mountains, sunset. (4) Simons. Harbor scene. (5) Simons. Cathedral, stone bridge. (6) Village, plumage. (Gold band.)

Fourth row: (1) House, mountains. (2) House, arched bridge. (3) Three houses in medallions. (4) Ornate rim. Castles. (5) Castles. (6) Buildings in circles. (Silver.)

Fifth row: (1) Houses. Coin silver. (2) Camels, palm trees. UR. (3) Houses, mountains. Beaded rim. (4) House, palm trees. (5) City scene. (6) Houses, mountains.

Religious

Most thimbles with a religious background are modern.

Top row: (Left) Mary. (Middle) Holy Family. (Right) Jesus.

Second row: (1) Last Supper. Made in Israel. (2) Panoramic view of Bethlehem. (3) Crusaders, copied from cathedral door. (4) Jerusalem. (5) Wailing Wall, Jerusalem.

Third row: (1) Nativity scene. (2) St. Peter's, Rome. (3) Pope John Paul II. Welcome to America 1979. (4) St. Bartholomew's fourteenth century church, Schoonhoven, Holland, Christmas 1979. (5) "Do unto others as you would have them do unto you."

Fourth row: (1) "La Conception." Italian. (2) Children's vision. Recordacao de N S de Fatima. (3) Mother Seton. Commemorates canonization. (4) Shrine of Fatima. Recordacao Basilica de Fatima. (5) Saint Teresa.

Fifth row: (1) "Serve the Lord with Gladness," Psalms 100.2. Blue plastic. (2) "Christ died for me." Aluminum, blue top. (3) "Jesus Cares." Aluminum. (4) "Jesus Never Fails." Aluminum, orange top. (5) "We walk by Faith not by Sight," Corinthians 5:7. Blue plastic.

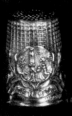

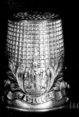
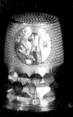

Enamel Thimbles

Enameled jewelry and thimbles have been made for centuries. A few early items exist but modern examples are beautiful and plentiful.

Top row: (1) Border with blue Greek key, amethyst top. (2) Simons, red band. (3) Flowered band, aqua with red roses. (4) Flowered white with pink roses. (5) Simons, pink and white band.

Second row: (1) Simons, light blue, pink roses. (2) Brass, white with flowered band. (3) Black with dogwood. (4) Cream colored floral bouquet. (5) Simons, yellow and white band, pink, blue flowers.

Third row: (1) Gabler, light blue, pink flowers. (2) Germany, aqua, pink roses scattered, stone top. (3) Gabler, black enamel, rose. (4) Simons, white enamel, pink roses. (5) Green chain design, green stone top.

Fourth row: (1) Pale blue, moonstone top. (2) Royal blue, moonstone top. (3) Copper, yellow enameling with birds and rushes. (4) Tropical scene, moonstone top. (5) Silver, blue, and white enamel bands, moonstone top.

Fifth row: (1) White, butterflies and flowers. (2) Christmas scene, blue, "Peace on Earth" on back. (3) Simons, light blue, roses on band. (4) White, bird on branch. (5) Copper color, large flowers.

Porcelains

Porcelain thimbles are collectible more for their beauty as souvenirs than for usefulness. Porcelains add color and art to displays.

Top row: (1) Mason's Patent Ironstone. England. (2) Kaiser, Johann Seltmann, West Germany. (3) Wales. GSM Bone china. Abermordou. (4) Rose. Aynsley, china. England. (5) Hand-painted. Herend. Hungary.

Second row: (1) Shamrocks. Bone china. Sandford, England. (2) Shamrock Dresden thimble. Made in Ireland. (3) "July" Maruri Masterpiece. Bone china. (4) Holly. Fine bone china. Royal Grafton. England. (5) Caverswall. England.

Third row: (1) Hollohaza 1834. Hungary. (2) Lily of the Valley. Duchess bone china. England. (3) Fine bone china. England. (4) Haviland, Limoges, France. (5) Bouquet. Bilston and Battersea enamels. England.

Fourth row: (1) Cock. Haviland. Limoges, France. (2) Horse and rider. Limoges. France. (3) Radnor bone china. England. (4) Bee. Bernardaud. Limoges, France. (5) Porsgrund. Norway.

Fifth row: (1) Royal Windsor fine bone china. England. (2) Caverswall. England. (3) Golden Crown bone china. England. (4) Hammersley fine bone china. England. (5) Violet. Canadian Superior fine bone china. Canada.

Sixth row: (1) "Daughter," Ashleydale fine bone china. England. (2) Coalport Est. 1750. England. (3) Adderley bone china. England. (4) Cupid. Spode bone china. England. (5) Swan Boat, April 19, 1877, Boston. Caverswall. England.

Panels

Paneled patterns were popular around the turn of the century.

Top row: (1) Plume. (2) Leaf. (3) Flower. (4) Fly. (5) Bird.

Second row: (1) Simons. (2) Simons. (3) Gold band. Initial "M." (4) Stars and moon. (5) Diamond.

Third row: (1) Arches. (2) Swirls. (3) Gold with niello. (4) Simons. (5) (Gold) Simons. Initial "E."

Fourth row: (1) Muhr. (2) Simons. (3) Simons. Indented crescent. (4) Simons. Indented ovals. (5) Open end.

Borders

Borders of varying widths afford space for decoration including settings, enamel, and engraved designs.

Top row: (1) Goldsmith Stern, gold, bird and thistle. (2) Sterling, special cupid, initials "MHD." (3) Cupid faces around rim. (4) Cupids with wreath, Simons, patented Nov. 21, 1905. (5) Gold, KMD border of scrolls and diamond shapes. Initials "L.H."

Second row: (1) Scalloped border, 800, with shield. (2) Brass border with diamond shapes and flowers, top in squares. (3) Gold, border of leaves and diamond design. UR on top. (4) Simons, gold, small flowers with leaves. (5) Sterling with border of roses, scalloped rim, Atlantic Cable style.

Third row: (1) Sterling with scrolled band. (2) J. A. Henckel, sterling, oak leaf border, blue top. (3) Sterling, scalloped. (4) Sterling, Goldsmith Stern, inverted heart shaped design. (5) Sterling with large leaf.

Fourth row: (1) Sterling, Simons with scrolled border. (2) Sterling, daisies with ribbon bands entwined. (3) Scalloped rim, arches and trefoil. (4) Sterling, Simons, scrolled border. (5) Sterling, KMD, eagle with four stars at wing span.

Fifth row: (1) Sterling with band of flowers and scrolls. (2) Sterling with gold band of circles and loops, engraved "H.B." (3) Sterling, Simons, arches and trefoil. (4) Sterling, roses with three separate rows of vines. (5) Waite-Thresher, sterling, border of daisies.

Animals, Birds, Fish, Fowl

Animals, birds, fish, and fowl appeared on some early thimbles, notably Gabler Bros. designs.

Top row: (1) Man on donkey walking around border. Mexican silver. (2) Fish. Gabler enamel. (3) Four cats, two sitting, two standing. Gabler enamel. (4) Reindeer. (5) Fawn.

Second row: (1) Wolf. (2) Camel. (3) Buffalo, horses. (4) Cat. (5) Turtle, hare.

Third row: (1) Bluebirds. (2) Bluebird. (3) Seagull, made in Denmark. (4) Swallow, "Just a swallow from Capistrano, California." (5) Swan.

Fourth row: (1) Kitten. Portugal. (2) Clydesdale horses. (3) Cat, cow, dog. "Cat and fiddle . . ." (4) Dinosaur. Sinclair Oil advertisement. (5) Geese.

Fifth row: (1) Chickens and chicks. (2) Donkey. (3) Elephant. (4) Horse and buggy. (5) Horses and sleigh.

Variations of Indentations

Among indentations on thimbles, patterns may be round, square, hexagonal or honeycomb, teardrop, diamond-shaped, as well as floral or conventional design or combinations.

Top row: (1) Small daisy. (2) Diamond and triangle. (3) Stars. (4) Large leaf, dome top, hand punched curved panels top to bottom. (5) Snowflakes.

Second row: (1) Simons. Vermicelli. (2) English floral. Semi-precious stone top. (3) Mums. Dorcas. (4) Floral. Early Dorcas. C.H. (Charles Horner). (5) Floral and waffle.

Third row: (1) All over flowers. England. (2) Mums and dots. Two rows beading on border. (3) Fan pattern with petal-like border. (4) Circle-dot with swirls. (5) Plain border extends upward irregularly to swirl pattern.

Fourth row: (1) Simons. Gold. Vermicelli pattern. "Grandma." (2) Simons. Vermicelli. New. (3) Simons. Flower, vine, leaf. Beaded rim. (4) Simons. Vermicelli. Paneled rim. (5) All-over large mums. German.

Contemporary Thimbles

The Franklin Mint Corporation offers sets of thimbles in limited edition series in sterling silver and porcelain with 24K gold trims. Pictured at right is a representative selection from their "First Ladies of the U.S." series. Portraits appearing on each bone china thimble were created by an artist-designer commissioned by the Franklin Mint, and the designs are exclusively copyrighted by the company. Photograph courtesy of the Franklin Mint Corporation.

Contemporary Thimbles

"The Country Store Thimbles" is a limited edition series which was offered to collectors by the Franklin Mint in 1980. Twenty-five different designs, each hand-decorated in 24K gold on porcelain, comprise the series. Each thimble bears an original design created exclusively for the collection. Photograph courtesy of the Franklin Mint Corporation.

© 1980 FP

Contemporary Thimbles

Pictured opposite is the Franklin Mint limited edition, "13 Colonies Thimbles." Crafted in sterling silver, each original design is banded by the name of the commonwealth. This is now a closed edition. Photograph courtesy of the Franklin Mint Corporation.

Swedish Colony

1638 – 1655

Bronze and brass thimbles discovered at various depths during excavations near Jamestown, Virginia. A Swedish colony existed on Tinicum Island from 1638 to 1655.

Names

A name engraved on a thimble identifies a treasured keepsake.

Top row: (1) "Carol," Simons, raised grape. (2) "Maud, June 27, 1906," gold, ornate edge. (3) "Annie," gold with scalloped border. (4) "Gladys," gold, scenic. (5) "Idabelle," gold.

Second row: (1) "Rita." (2) "Nettie." (3) "Bess." (4) "Edith," ten panels. (5) "Loraine," aster in ovals.

Third row: (1) "Lina." (2) "Diane." (3) "Tina." (4) "Lisa." (5) "Sharon."

Fourth row: (1) "Nancie," scenic. (2) "Grace." (3) "Sara," cathedral windows with beaded rim. (4) "Eva, Dec. '86." (5) "Teresa," Santa Teresa, Spain.

Fifth row: (1) "Lucile," 21 cherub faces on border. Goldsmith-Stern Co. (2) "Alma." (3) "May," half-star and berry border. (4) "Carrie." (5) "Abbie."

Ketcham & McDougall Thimblemakers

1832 to 1932

Thimbles photographed are from the combined collections of Leona Mach Coad and Sandra Froehlich McFadyen.

Style identification compiled by Leona Mach Coad and Sandra Froehlich McFadyen directly from original KMD catalogs and price lists.

Written information compiled by Sandra Froehlich McFadyen and taken from KMD catalogs and price lists, and the 125th Anniversary book printed by the Firm in 1957, entitled "The Story Behind 'Since 1832' . . . the 125 years of Ketcham & McDougall, Inc."

> "The betrothal thimble is now — in the modern
> Ketcham & McDougall, Inc. plant at Roseland,
> New Jersey, as in the average American home —
> merely a nostalgic reminder of bygone days."
> (Quoted from 125th Anniversary Book.)

Ketcham & McDougall made thousands of thimbles over a period of one hundred years. The company is still in business but thimbles have not been made since 1932.

1832   John Roshore, New York.

1834   Moved to 6 Little Green Street. Edward Ketcham became his apprentice. A few years later, Hugh McDougall, who was an apprentice in a jewelry shop in Huntington, Long Island, came to the city and began working for Roshore and Ketcham.

1850s   Roshore retired; Edward Ketcham's brother, E. P., joined Firm; Firm became Ketcham and Brother.

1876   Renamed Firm Ketcham and McDougall; Location: Manhattan.

1880s   Relocated in Brooklyn.

1886   Hugh McDougall's son, Walter, joined Firm. Early 1900s, moved from downtown Broadway to Silversmith's Building on Maiden Lane; stayed here until 1931.

After World War I, Ketcham family, Walter and Charles, sons of Hugh McDougall, changed old partnership into a corporation under New York State law with Walter McDougall as president.

1932   Thimblemaking discontinued.

Miscellaneous Information

Addresses: 37 and 39 Maiden Lane (date unknown)

1917 – not incorporated, 15, 16, 17 Maiden Lane

1921 – incorporated, 15, 16, 17 Maiden Lane

1924 – incorporated, 15 Maiden Lane

Rare Thimble Style Descriptions

Cherubs — 14K Style #80, 10K Style #080.

Stitch in Time — Sterling Style #184.

Lily of the Valley — Sterling Style #119.

Dog's Head — 14K Style #81, 10K Style #081 (Note: This thimble has Louis XV edge)

Listed on a 1917 Price List is Style #64, 14K with pearls and turquoises.

Engine turned thimbles were made in sterling, sterling/gold banded, 10K, 14K, and 14K green gold.

Children's thimbles were made in sizes 1 to 4.

Ketcham and McDougall

Top row: (1) Sterling, Style #136, Louis XV, heavy weight. Note that the thimble pictured has been deliberately cut off. There is no evidence that KMD made this style in an open top. (2) Sterling, Style 136, Louis XV, heavy weight, not cut off. KMD made this style in sterling with an enameled band style 136E and in sterling, enameled, and gilt band Style 136EG. (3) Sterling, Style #132, Knurled to Rim, heavy weight. KMD made an open top style 157 — style 157L indicated large sizes. (4) Sterling, Style #105, Plain, heavy weight (older). KMD made an open top style 122. (5) Sterling, Style #105, Plain, heavy weight (newer). This thimble design replaced design shown in thimble 4 on this row. (6) Sterling, Style #108, Chased, bright cut, heavy weight. KMD made an open top style 123. Also shown in catalog are landscapes with same edge, no bright cut, 108L and open top 123L.

Second row: (1) Sterling, Style #167, Renaissance, medium weight. (2) Sterling, Style #139, Panelled, heavy weight. (3) Sterling, Style #163, Wild Rose, French grey, heavy weight. KMD made a 10K, rose colored gold band style 164. (4) Sterling, Style #150, Damask, flowered, medium weight or Style #151 same description only heavy weight. KMD made an open top style 124. (5) Sterling, Style #103, Plain, medium weight. (6) Sterling variation of Style #103. KMD made an open top style #121.

Third row: (1) Sterling, Style #149, Embossed Scroll, heavy weight. KMD also made Style 149G same description, French grey. (2) Sterling, Style #144, Embroidery, Louis XV edge, extra heavy weight. (3) Sterling, Style #137, Chased Scroll, extra heavy weight. (4) Sterling, Style #142, Chased, round rim, medium weight or Style #140 same description only heavy weight. (5) Sterling, Style #107, Chased, bright cut, medium weight. (6) Sterling, Style #143, Chased, scroll, heavy weight.

Fourth row: (1) Sterling, Style #129, Fluted, heavy weight. (2) Sterling, Style #110, Faceted, heavy weight. (3) Sterling, Style #106, Plain, extra heavy weight. (4, 5, 6) Three thimbles are all variations of description that follows: Sterling, Style #114, Engraved Band, heavy weight.

Fifth row: (1) Sterling, Style #107, described Row 3, #5. (2) Sterling, Style #231, Fluted, gold 10K band, extra heavy weight. (3, 4, 5, 6) All variations of description that follows: Sterling, Style #148, gold 10K band, extra heavy weight or Sterling, Style #112, gold 14K band, extra heavy weight. Style numbers vary because of gold content. It is difficult to identify this type of

engraved scroll-type banded thimble unless thimble is clearly
marked 10K or 14K on band. Styles of bands differed depend-
ing on who made the engraving and the technique used in making the thimble. A collector may also compare the gold values
of other marked thimbles. There is a difference in color.

Ketcham and McDougall

Top row: (1) Style #160, Scroll, gold 10K band, heavy weight or Style #161, Scroll, gold 14K band, rose colored, heavy weight. (2) Style #231, described on other photo, Row 5, #2. (3 and 4) Next two thimbles are either Style #148 or #112. Detailed description on other photo Row 5, #3, 4, 5 and 6.

Second row: (1) Style #164, Wild Rose, gold 10K band, rose colored, extra heavy weight. Note that there is no evidence of a 14K band. (2) Sterling, gold band. (3) 10K, Style #075, Square panels (14K is Style 75) marked. (4) 14K, Style #67, Paneled (no evidence of 10K) marked.

Third row: (1) 10K, Style #31, Chased or 14K Style #41, Chased Edge. Thimble pictured is marked only with an "o." There is no conclusive evidence of what the "o" means. This may be a mark for 10K. Most KMD 10K style numbers have an "o" in front of the same style numbers for the 14K thimbles. (2) 10K, Style #30, Chased Edge or 14K, Style #40, Chased. The thimble pictured is marked only with an "o." (3) 10K, Style #30X, Chased Edge. Marked. (4) 14K, Style #79, Double Bead Edge (10K is Style 079). Marked. (5) 14K, Style #76, Bead Edge (10K is Style 076). Marked. (6) 14K, Style #70, Chased Round Edge (10K is style 070). Marked.

Fourth row: (1) 14K, Style #52, Plain Facet (10K is style 052). Marked. (2) 14K Green Gold, Style #91G, Engine Turned (10K is style 091, 14K is style 91). Green gold is not listed in a 1917 price list but is added in the 1921 price list as costing 25¢ extra. (3) 10K, Style #043, Plain Band or 14K, Style #43, Plain Band Thimble pictured is marked only with an "o." (4) 10K, Style #063, Fluted or 14K, Style #63, Fluted. Thimble pictured is marked only with an "o." (5) This thimble is Marked 14K but catalogs show only the 10K Style #38. Engraved band. (6) 14K, Style #68, Louis XV (10K is style 068). Marked. KMD made thi 14K thimble with an enameled band, Style 68E.

Fifth row: (1, 2, 3) The first three thimbles are described as follows: 10K, Style #073, Embossed Scroll or 14K, Style #73, Embossed Scroll (1) Marked only with an "o"; (2) No markings, amethyst was added later and is not an original thimble style. (3) Marked 14K. (4) 10K, Style #057, Chased Band, beaded edge or 14K, Style #57, Chased band, beaded edge. Thimble pictured is marked only with an "o." (5) 10K, Style #089, Wild Rose, rose finish band or 14K, Style #89, Wild Rose, rose finish. Thimble pictured is marked only with an "o." (6) 10K, Style #071, Chased Scroll (14K is Style 71). Marked.

Rare Thimbles

(1) French, eighteenth century, gold with so-called wedding ring motif. (2, 3, 4) The three parts of an extremely rare sixteenth century German composite thimble. The silver gilt inner part (shown at center) carries a "maker's mark" and enameled entwined coats of arms in the top. The filigree enameled "outer ring" and the top part form the "outer thimble"; they are shown to the left and the right, respectively, of the "inner thimble." The complete thimble is shown in photo II. (5) Gold, art nouveau thimble with beautifully engraved border showing girls sewing. This thimble was designed by Frenchman Vernon.

(1) Dutch, seventeenth century silver thimble carrying the Amsterdam hallmark. The "chasing animals" border motif is typical. (2) Dutch, eighteenth century silver open sewing ring, showing identical border as the one in II-1. (3) German, sixteenth century composite thimble (See Photo I). (4) Dutch, seventeenth century brass sailor's sewing ring recovered from the Dutch ship "Hollandia" which sank off the Scilly Islands in 1743. (5) Dutch, nineteenth century silver thimble carrying the inscription "Vaarwel, vergeet mij niet" (Farewell, do not forget me) between a double border row of stars.

The above photographs are used through the courtesy of Cecile Dreesmann, artist, and Dutch celebrity whose "Needlesculptures" made of free hand embroidery with gold, minerals, and precious stones are collector's items not only in her own country but in the United States, England, France, and Germany to name a few. Mrs. Dreesmann has been interested in thimble history for nearly thirty years. She says she is fascinated by the diversity and incredibly many different forms this small utilitarian object has taken.

Dorcas Thimbles

Dorcas thimbles are made of steel sandwiched between a silver lining and an outside layer of silver for durability.

Decorative indentations on most Dorcas thimbles enhance the designs. Dreema is a style also made with steel interlining.

Early Dorcas thimbles were not marked but resemble later ones bearing a rectangle with "Dorcas" and "C.H." for Charles Horner.

A magnet will attract steel to verify the content.

"Dorcas" was the name chosen from the biblical story of the woman who sewed for the poor. Church sewing groups are sometimes called Dorcas societies.

Part Three

Contemporary Thimbles

"Modern thimbles will be the heirlooms of tomorrow."

Selections of modern thimbles are sold by most gift stores. Airport shops offer a variety of souvenir thimbles for travelers.

Beautiful bone china thimbles lend color to a collection. Sterling and gold as remembrances are much appreciated.

Mail order catalogs advertise hundreds of thimbles for all occasions, seasons, or holiday displays.

Limited Editions

Sets of limited editions of 5000 are offered by The Franklin Mint, Franklin Center, Pennsylvania. Among these are the First Ladies, Garden Birds, Butterflies and Flowers in porcelain. The Thirteen Colonies, limited to 5000, are sterling. (See photographs pp. 41-45.)

Collector's Choice, Lake Park, Florida, offers a limited edition of twenty Heroines of History. Individual thimbles, Pope John Paul II, Hawaii State Flower, and annual issues of memorable occasions, by Hurley artists and Marihelen Engelen, are limited editions.

Also by Collector's Choice: A "Day of the Week" set of seven pewter thimbles, illustrating "Monday's Child . . ." and so forth. A set of 53 pewter thimbles for every state in the Union, Washington, D.C., Canada, and Puerto Rico, is American made.

Downs' Collectors Showcase, Milwaukee, Wisconsin, offers limited editions of individual Porsgrund (Norway) and Kaiser (West Germany) thimbles. A series is offered of handcrafted bone china classical ballerinas, sold individually.

Lillian Vernon's Country Gourmet catalog, Mount Vernon, New York offers exclusive thimbles from Scotland, England, Austria, West Germany, Italy, and Spain.

Harriet Carter's catalog, Plymouth Meeting, Pennsylvania, offers Mother of Pearl on copper, sandalwood, ceramic Irish blessings, bone china dog, and other animal thimbles.

Taylor Gifts, Wayne, Pennsylvania, advertises Irish Dresden thimbles, Coca Cola thimble of ruby glass, carnation thimble of bread dough, hand-painted robin, bluebird, or butterflies.

Yield House, North Conway, New York advertises thimbles of Mother of Pearl from Philippines, jade from Taiwan, brass from India, silver plate from India, cloisonne from Taiwan, and hand-blown fluted edge glass thimbles made in the United States.

Unique Products, Callicoon, New York, offers filigree, sterling with abalone insets, and designs of sterling thimbles.

Thimbletter

Another source of thimbles is the "Leads" column in Thimbletter, a newsletter for thimble collectors, by Lorraine Crosby, Newton Highlands, Massachusetts.

(Note: The sources mentioned suggest only a few of the places thimbles are available)

Plastic Thimbles

Plastic thimbles provide many categories. It would be challenging to acquire 1000 plastic thimbles with different indentations, width of borders, and colors.

It might also be possible to accumulate 1000 personal thimbles, bearing the name, address, or other personal identification.

Advertising

Advertising thimbles bearing names, places, and services are available in plastic, aluminum, nickel, silver, and various other materials. Subgroups of specific enterprises or industries are frequently classified.

Contemporary Thimbles

The following limited editions of thimbles are available from Collector's Choice, 1313 S. Killian Drive, Lake Park, Florida 33403.

Top row: Heroines of History: (1) Mary Queen of Scots. (2) Elizabeth I of England. (3) Helen of Troy. (4) Isabella of Spain. (5) Catherine of Russia.

Second row: Heroines of History: (1) Joan of Arc. (2) Tzu Hsi, Empress of China. (3) Eleanor Roosevelt, U.S.A.
(The entire collection of 20 Heroines of History thimbles is available from Collector Circle. Above address.)

Third row: (1) Pope John Paul II. Limited to 5000. (2) Clown. Hand-painted by Hurley artists. (3) Hawaii state flower. Hurley. (4) Christmas 1980. Annual edition by Hurley. (5) Moscow Olympics 1980. Limited number issued. Production halted because of boycott.

Fourth row: (1) Christmas in Sweden. (2) Christmas in Germany. (3) Christmas in Mexico. (4) 1980 Mother's Day, handpainted by Hurley. (5) 1980 Grandparents Day. Hurley.

Fifth row: (1, 2, and 3) Kittens, handpainted by Marihelen Engelen. (4) Dream Angel. Limited to 1000. Handpainted by Marihelen. (5) Santa Mouse. Limited to 1000. Handpainted by Marihelen.

Simons Bros. Co.
SINCE 1839
214 South 12th St., Phila., Pa. 19107

STERLING SILVER THIMBLES

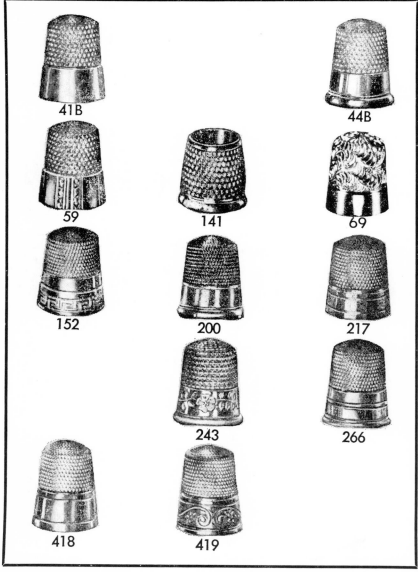

41B

44B

59

141

69

152

200

217

243

266

418

419

200 GOLD FILLED   **418 AND 419 GOLD BAND**

62

10 KT. AND 14 KT. GOLD THIMBLES

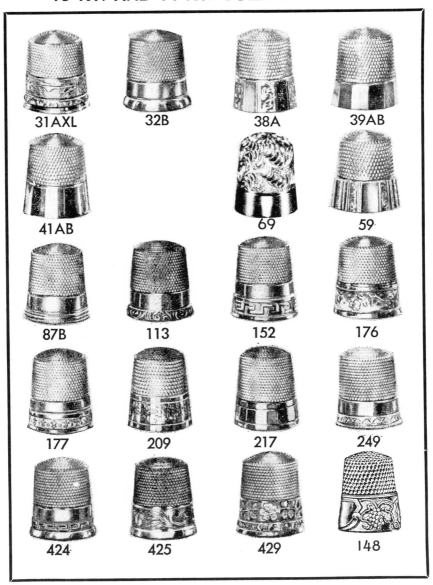

31AXL   32B   38A   39AB

41AB   69   59

87B   113   152   176

177   209   217   249

424   425   429   148

Part Four
Thimble Trademarks and Patents

"Trademark" represents a name, symbol, or mark used by a manufacturer or merchant to identify his products. A trademark does not necessarily refer to the maker. These are usually registered, the first in this country having been entered in 1871. Again, a certain fine quality of manufacture is assigned to the product by a well-reputed trademark.

Many silversmiths had brought their talents from European countries. There were no trade schools. Young men served long apprenticeships, often from 14 to 21 years of age, to master silversmiths. After serving their time, they frequently went into business for themselves or into partnership with another smith.

A.D. 1693 . . . . N° 319.

Engine for Making Thimbles.

LOFTING'S PATENT.

WILLIAM AND MARY, by the grace of God, &c., to all to whome these presents shall come, greeting.

WHEREAS JOHN LOFTING hath, by his humble peticōn, represented vnto vs that the great dutys charged vpon all thimbles imported from beyond the
5 seas doth much discourage the merchants from bringing the same over, soe that the price of that cōmodity will come to be enhansed vpon our subiects, and that in Germany and other forreigne parts whence they have been heretofore imported into this kingdome they are vsually made by a certaine engine or instrument hitherto vnknowne in our dominions, and hath humbly prayed vs
0 to grant him our Letters Patents for the sole priviledge of makeing and selling the said engine or instruement.

KNOW YEE THEREFORE, that wee, being graciously pleased to condescend to that his request, of our especiall grace, certaine knowledge, and meer moōn, have given and granted, and by these presents, for vs, our heires and
5 successors, doe give and grant vnto the said John Loftingh, his executors, administrators, and assignes, speciall lycence, full power, sole priviledge and authority, that he, the said John Loftingh, his executors, administrators, and assignes, and every of them, by themselves or his or their deputy and deputies, servants or agents, or such others as the said John Loftingh, his executors, administrators, or assignes, shall at any time agree with, and noe others, from time to time and at all times dureing the terme of yeares herein expressed, shall and lawfully may make, sell, and enioy the said engine or instrument for " MAKING THIMBLES FOR MEN, WOMEN, AND CHILDREN," within any part or

the said engine or instruement, or the materialls thereto conduceing and belonging.

In witnesse, &c. Witnesse ourselves at Westminster, the Fourth day of April. *(1693)*
By Writt of Privy Seale.

LONDON:
Printed by GEORGE EDWARD EYRE and WILLIAM SPOTTISWOODE,
Printers to the Queen's most Excellent Majesty. 1857.

DESIGN.

H. A. WEIHMAN.

THIMBLE.

No. 22,547.

Patented June 20, 1893.

FIG. 1.

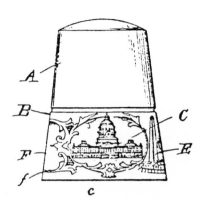

FIG. 2.

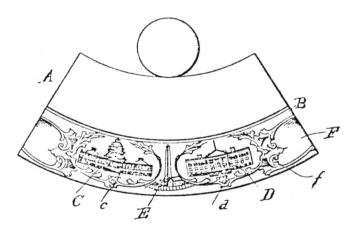

WITNESSES:

Henry Drury

INVENTOR:

Henry A. Weihman
By his attorney,

DESIGN.

No. 37,680.

PATENTED NOV. 21, 1905.

H. A. WEIHMAN.
THIMBLE.
APPLICATION FILED FEB. 7, 1905.

FIG.1

FIG.2

INVENTOR

Henry A. Weihman

BY

Attorney

WITNESSES:
M. C. Eyre.
Jean / Almey.

DESIGN.

J. F. SIMONS.
THIMBLE.

No. 28,721.

Patented May 31, 1898.

FIG. 1

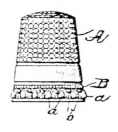

FIG. 2

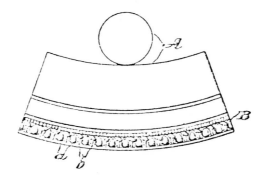

Witnesses.

Inventor

John. F. Simons

By

Attorney.

68

C. HORNER.
THIMBLE.

No. 404,910.   Patented June 11, 1889.

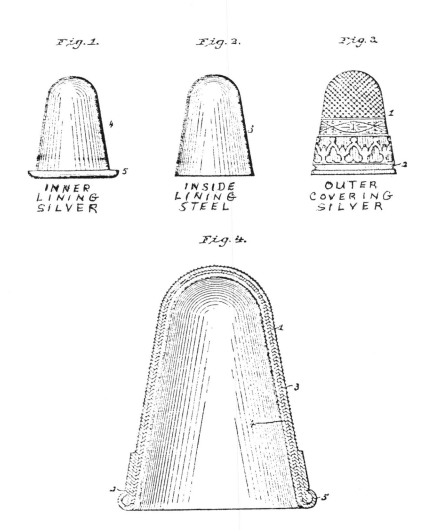

Fig. 1.

INNER
LINING
SILVER

Fig. 2.

INSIDE
LINING
STEEL

Fig. 3.

OUTER
COVERING
SILVER

Fig. 4.

WITNESSES:

INVENTOR:
By his Attorneys,

Thomas S. Brogan
New York, N. Y.

Charles Horner
England

Gabler Bros.
Germany
Some slight variations.
See Proctor thimble tops.

Stern Bros. Co.
New York, N. Y.
(Later with Goldsmith Stern Company.)

Goldsmith Stern Company
New York, N. Y.

NICKEL

Simons Bros.   Philadelphia, Pa.
Many variations.

H. Muhr Sons
Philadelphia, Pa.

Webster Company
North Attelboro, Mass.

Waite-Thresher Co.
Providence, R. I.
(Early mark a star.)
Barker Manufacturing Company
(Also used star.)
(Later part of Waite-Thresher Company)

Waite-Thresher Company
(Later mark)
(When Waite-Thresher Company went
out of business. Simons Bros.
bought designs)

Index

For Reference

Previous volumes by the same author, *The Book of a Thousand Thimbles*, 1970, (Book 1), and *Thimble Treasury*, 1975, (Book 2), Wallace-Homestead Book Co.

Book 1

Book 2